ONE AND HALF OF YOU

ALSO BY LEANNE DUNIC

The Gift

To Love the Coming End

one
and
half
of
you

leanne dunic

TALONBOOKS

Talonbooks
9259 Shaughnessy Street, Vancouver, British Columbia, Canada V6P 6R4
talonbooks.com

Talonbooks is located on xʷməθkʷəy̓əm, Sḵwx̱wú7mesh, and səl̓ilwətaʔɬ
Lands.

First printing: 2021

Typeset in Minion
Printed and bound in Canada on 100% post-consumer recycled paper

Interior and cover design by andrea bennett
Cover image by Katie So

Talonbooks acknowledges the financial support of the Canada Council
for the Arts, the Government of Canada through the Canada Book Fund,
and the Province of British Columbia through the British Columbia Arts
Council and the Book Publishing Tax Credit.

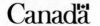  

LIBRARY AND ARCHIVES CANADA CATALOGUING IN PUBLICATION

Title: One and half of you : poems / Leanne Dunic.
Names: Dunic, Leanne, author.
Identifiers: Canadiana 20200406949 | ISBN 9781772012866 (softcover)
Classification: LCC PS8607.U535 O54 2021 | DDC C811/.6—dc23

For the ones I love

I

Music to accompany Section I, "Nostalgia Distorts":
talonbooks.com/OAHOY ♪

First, there were them, and them, and them.
Then more. Faces mixed. A pocket here, a
clan there. Landscapes shifted – people, too.
Communities disappeared.

And now there is me. I will draw you some maps.

Birthmarks: some have vanished, but then
again, nostalgia distorts.

Sometimes I forget that I'm Chinese.

That I'm not.

I have
two halves

mountains   I try
        to move

Sometimes,   I'm not level
and   my wine spills

What does   this mean
for making a   point?

Dangerous between   unless
you   are   the   mover

Slow   slow   crumbs

        of   earth

        elevation

in   my

hands

My zodiac: dog.

Part pug? Shih Tzu? Pekingese? Definitely
of Chinese descent.

Our home was across from the Tsartlip*
reserve, where the Sam kids lived. My
mother has the same surname but is a
different colour. Our families are connected
by this road that divides us.

As a child, I didn't understand the history of
this land, that gathering clams and sea beans
from the shores was stealing.

---

*   W̱JOȽEȽP

Elementary school. Recesses are
inquisitions. <Are you Indian?>

Unclear what exactly <Indian> means.
Barely understand <Eurasian>, a word my
mother taught me while holding a globe,
pointing to the ridges of Yugoslavia, the
mass that was China.

Europe. Asia.

Europe Asia. Canada.

Eurasian.

Canadian.

You.

Mother, disowned by her own for marrying
a white man.

My brother doesn't look distinctly Chinese or Croatian, though he has our paternal grandfather's solemn, long-lashed eyes.

<Those halfers are always so good-looking.>

In America, passersby call my brother
<Elvis>. Cops call him < ■■ >.†

Friends call him <Chinatown>.

---

†   An offensive slur that pheneticized him as Hispanic.

His interests: the car he drives, the girl on his arm.

The girl will never be Asian. *They remind me too much of you.*

My brother's zodiac: he doesn't know.
(Rat.)

In the grass, I find one. Young. Eyes open.
Bottom half missing, a tangle of still-moist
intestine wrapped behind what's left of its
back. Fur is damp as if it has been
affectionately licked.

A girl in my kindergarten class remembers
me as the girl who had a crush on the
Ghostbusters.

I loved them all, but especially Harold
Ramis as Egon Spengler. Not only was he
handsome, he was smart. He became my
attraction prototype: glasses, intelligence,
Adam's apple.

Funny that the girl from my kindergarten
class remembers my Ghostbuster-crush
more than me kissing her nearly every day.
When I think of her, that's what I remember.

My neighbours had blue eyes and light-
blond hair and took me to worship with
them once a week. I prayed to their god,
giving him an ultimatum that if he was real,
he'd make me blond like my Barbie doll.
Blond like the girls I kissed in class.

During Christmas break, we'd watch
The Nutcracker on TV. Of course, my
brother pretended he was the Rat King. I
hoped for my own whiteness and a prince to
take me to other worlds.

Games passed down from our parents: a box
of Tressette cards and a jewelled cookie tin
full of mah-jong tiles. We didn't know how
to play with either.

Back then, I believed the voice on the radio
was Neil *Yeung* and that Pearl S. Buck was
Chinese.

Rat and I played where freshwater flowed
into the Saanich Inlet‡ – mixed salinity. Here
life evolved to endure movement between:
fresh to salt, wet to dry, warm to cold, land
to sea.

Rippling in the ocean-bound creek, the
largest snake we'd ever seen. It twisted in
my grasp until its jaw took hold of my hand.

---

‡   S̱NIDȻEȽ

At recess, the older kids taunted, <Are you a boy or a girl?> I was pretty sure I was a girl but didn't understand why I wanted to kiss boys *and* girls when I knew I wasn't supposed to. Gender didn't matter. Age didn't either; I recall not just kissing my classmates, but the grey-haired school principal too. I loved to love.

Victoria's nineteenth-century
red-light district is now Market Square:
fuchsia baskets, a fudge shop,
and twenty-five-cent mechanical horse rides.

There, as a child, Rat saw ghosts. I felt it
too. Something of our history was here, but
all we knew was inherited sadness.

In my young sleep, souls came unbidden,
passing through my body as a shiver.

His BMW totalled, Rat called at midnight
from the hospital crying, *I don't think I can
ever drive again.*

But here he is, a week later, twenty-three years old,
with the shiny, red, growling car he's
wanted *ever since I was young.*

The Ferrari was trailered from California to
British Columbia. It's never seen a day of
rain in its life, and to keep it that way, Rat
buses to work.

I have recurring dreams of driving a manual
transmission. Of revving engines.

We were students at a Chinese school in a
classroom mobile.

一

二

三

I longed to attend the Chinese Public School
on Fisgard Street. Cinnamon-coloured
bricks, tiered, tiled roof – a temple.

水

金

山

After a year of Saturdays we were pulled
out. No more writing   right

to left.

Mother said, *We speak Cantonese, not
Mandarin.*

And now I speak neither.

Driving me to my (girl)friend's house my
dad asked, "You're not gay, are you?"

Maybe I had borrowed his clothes too often.
Or maybe it was the short hair.

Classmates called me <dyke>. It didn't help
that I went to the Melissa Etheridge concert
where I bought a bandana covered in
Venus symbols (*Your Little Secret* tour).
When someone commented on how lesbian
it was, I didn't know what to do with the
shame, or the bandana.

My first apartment was in the Chung Wah
Mansion on Herald Street,
Chinatown, the ghosts
of Market Square only blocks away.

Honeysuckle wood trim.
The fifth-floor deck peeked at
the Chinese Public School.

Further from youth, yet closer, too.

Rat said, *I will never live in an apartment
with advertisements in the elevator.*

From the age of twelve, Rat worked as a
paperboy, dishwasher, cook – all to buy a
car at fifteen years old. Father had to drive it
home. Once he turned sixteen, he could
work as a pizza delivery boy, too.

I'll let you punch me in the stomach if you
let me press my ear to your heart.

No.

High school: one other Asian – a Japanese
girl. We watched boys lust for fresh-breasted
white girls. My crush called me <Karate Kid>.

Abnormally tall for my age, for a girl, for
someone with Asian genes. Boys don't want
to be with girls who loom.

New to school, a Russian exchange student
with a military haircut and a virgin
moustache. He was the one who *did* like me.
Me, one of the few who made nothing of his
ignorance of the Western high-school dress
code.

After Christmas break, the moustache
disappeared. A new haircut, a new
wardrobe, new friends, and a girlfriend with
straight brown hair and gold highlights.

As a late teen at a concert, a girl grabbed me
by my studded belt and pulled me to her. We
made out behind the venue. It took a few
more women to grab me by the belt.

I lived in the Chung Wah Mansion with a
girl with glacier-fair skin, icicle eyes, hair as
black as night. She and I met at the
restaurant where we worked. There, men in
their late twenties flirted with a fifteen-year-
old Filipina busser. They were more insistent
with me, a couple of years older.

Men loved seeing my roommate and me together.
This fetishization scared me. She used to
pride herself on her lack of emotion, but
when I told her I was moving in with a man,
her tears were relentless.

While our parents were out, Rat showed me
a video that took hours to download via dial-
up. Pamela Anderson and Tommy Lee on a
boat.

On sunny days, Rat picks me up in his
Ferrari, the engine vibrating the windows of
my house. I bend into the low car. He
accelerates before my seatbelt is latched and
I shriek: half irritation, half thrill. He stops
hard, turns fast. The more upset I get the
more he laughs.

On Granville Street, he nearly hits a
pedestrian trying to cross. I scold him. He
gives me his pouty, I'm-sorry-sister look but
I'm furious. I fear his belief that he won't
live beyond thirty. A silent scream: Don't
you know how much I love you?

When we still bathed together, Rat showed
me his baby-skinned erection.
This means I love you.

Multiple times, hands around Rat's throat,
kicks to his stomach and groin.

Now, we're grown.

I dwell in the Chinatowns of port cities.
Victoria, Vancouver, stints in Singapore,
Kobe, Yokohama, San Francisco, Seattle.
No answers, only red and gold plastic
decorations and the question, <Is your
mother Chinese?>

They never ask if it's my father who's
Chinese.

At the till of Chinatown Supermarket on
Keefer Street, I'm sick, voiceless. Shopping
basket holds ginger, choy sum, sachima, laap
cheung.

In Cantonese, the clerk yells, <Check out
this beautiful girl up front!>

<Bet her mother is Chinese.>

<Yes, the mother.>

I nod. Try to express understanding. They
don't notice.

Men from the backroom casually come to
the counter.

<Isn't she beautiful?>

I hold my hand to my throat.

They don't understand.

Wayson Choy's *The Jade Peony*. A Chinese
Canadian author. An invitation to
community I didn't know I lacked. To
possibilities.

Wong Kar-Wai's *In the Mood for Love*. I
become obsessed with vintage cheongsams.
Want to be wrecked by love.

Price depends on how the cheongsam
was made, the fabric used.

Gasp. Lift breasts with one hand.
Stuff your body inside.

If *you* wear this print of peonies
people may call them cabbages.

Hand-sewn, it's vulnerable to tears.
A machine can fix that.

Needles pinned will prick as you slip out
try another.

This dress – too loose.
Take in the back, add darts in the front
(though the fit will clearly be forced).

Wear this one of tangerine wool
high collar, tapered sleeves.

Double-lined
it will cost more to reshape.

Change the zipper to invisible.

Create the illusion
you
were born with this
as skin.

My legs, the ones that make me a tower –
attractive in one sense, intimidating in
another.

Modelling agencies in Japan reject me for
looking <too Asian>, desire blue
eyes, childlike features. I end up in
Singapore where I am called <model>
everywhere I go. Never beautiful, only
model.

I turn off the flight map, our dot somewhere
over the Pacific Ocean. Try to invoke sleep
until ...

<Excuse me, are you Indian?>

What?

<There's no nose like yours in Asia – maybe
in India.>

I'm half-Chinese, but the nose is Croatian.

<It's what?>

Croatian.

<Hmm?>

Former Yugoslavia.

(Shakes head.)

Europe.

<Germany?>

Less than twenty-four hours after landing in
Singapore, at the *For Him Magazine*
headquarters:

<I know you.>

Impossible.

<You're his sister.>

(A model Rat dated for a weekend.)

<How's he doing?>

Happenstance moves us into the same
housing a week later. She sits at the edge of
my bunk bed. <How's your brother?>

Her: the blondest blond, pixie nose, cat
eyes.

Her model boyfriend: a Filipino rendition of
my brother.

From Vancouver to this equatorial island.

Between, shadows of clouds rest on the skin
of the Pacific.

        Ghost   isles.

Here, I don't belong. A snow crystal at
home, here I am condensation.

Here heat can prick.

II

Music to accompany Section II, "Yoyogi Park":
talonbooks.com/OAHOY ♫

I dream of the sea: keeper of bones, micro-plastics, absorber of light – sure of the distant wave, I stand in the shallows. The current silvers a dead perch. I want to peer beneath, even if I must face the sting. The sea pulls at my soles, pushes at my shins.

Mondays, Tuesdays, Wednesdays,
Thursdays, Fridays. On the B-line sits a man
my age who I feel is my brother. Besides his
mixed skin, he's nothing like my real
brother – awkwardly tall, quiet, glasses,
Adam's apple, hairless. No car, no blond
on his arm. He reads a book at the back of
the bus, never lifting his head to notice me
watching him, twisting the strap of my bag,
wondering how I can ask – no, tell – him we
are the same.

I take the bus to meet Rat for dim sum and
he's already polished off a steamer of sticky
rice and two orders of beef balls. One
shrimp dumpling remains in the bamboo
steamer. *Ha gaau?* he offers.

I'm allergic to seafood.

Oh yeah. His lips are greasy. His wallet sits
among a pile of napkins. *My Ferrari caught
fire, waiting for a flatbed to arrive. Siu maai?*

Rat tells me how a girl threw up on his cock
while giving him head. I tell him I once got
ejaculate in my eye.

I don't want to hear about you *having sex.*

Mother tells me that Rat's current non-Asian girlfriend, the blond model I lived with in Singapore, has said, <He loves his sister very much.>

Too often: my lanky counterpart, the same
path. Reading at the back of the bus.

Rat, when was the last time you were happy?

The first time I had a blow job.

How many years ago was that?

Actually, they've all been pretty good.

Even the pukey one?

A long-legged silhouette cycles towards me
as we pass beneath the Chinatown gate. His
limbs are like the frame of his bicycle, each
piece straight, slender.

I move to stand in his path. He slows before
me.

Now you will know me.

I've watched you for too long.

I dream of us together in a bathtub.

He found me in a slow stream. Algae circled
my calves. His chestnut eyes, bulbs to see a
thousand different views, wondered why I
crouched there.

I told him my affections sought tadpoles,
salamanders. I pointed to my bucket on the
embankment.

> *amphi*: of both kinds
> *bios*: life

We sat in the grass. My muddied feet dried,
flaked. I leaned against the hairless skin of
my amphibious twin.

Cheeks pink, his mouth parted for oxygen.
Sunlight auraed his oval skull, his frame
long like a flagellum.

Soft bodies darted against plastic walls.

His zodiac: he doesn't subscribe to mass
generalizations. (Snake.)

Two coiled together lengthwise. An
embrace, or stranglehold?

Do my brother and I look alike? He would say no, that I look like our mother.

Snake and I, we look alike. Both skinny and tall, the same oyster flesh that makes us look Chinese.

Both our mothers trace their lineage to Vancouver Island.

At the flea market, our fingers trace tables of renegade heirlooms. For the two of us. To make up for the years we weren't family.

Have you seen *In the Mood for Love*?

It's my favourite movie.

Eyes shut
remember childhood
sleeps. Recall his
presence years before
we knew each
other's scent. Imagine
the red when we peel
skins apart.

My mouth is a scallop agape
the underside of a cowrie.

Chinatown, four-by-ten room, the gap between
books. Paper and beeswax. Scent captive
like insects in resin. Selves we shelve for
future reference. Discover intimacy of sleep.
Difficult to catalogue, love is full of defiant
compulsions. Inhale. Wear it like rubies.

Unfold
between us
a chestnut.
Sprouting stem
pink tipped.

Nourish body, nourish spirit. Attract a lover, attract divinity.

When I was a kid, my relations shopped at the same butcher in Chinatown. Mounds of pig ears, chopped red and sticky, brown-paper-wrapped. Water chestnut, pomegranate, pomelo. Bins of autumn produce, bull-like caltrops, poisonous if undercooked. Wicked, bovine fruit. Crunch cartilage. Stew hard. Bone broth.

The restaurant's wallpaper is a photograph, a
garden faded to pastel. Succulent siu yuk
and si yau gai hang in the window.

Chinatown is dying. How to prepare?

From torn plastic menus, two cha siu rice
noodles in soup. The waitress mutters dialect
as she walks away.

Cantonese: my mother's muddled, his never
spoke a word.

Two tables away, an elderly couple rinse
chopsticks in tea.

                         Is that normal?

I shake my head.

           Will we do the same when we're old?

I click sticks between my fingers.

I don't even hold them properly.

Soup noodles arrive. We don't clean our chopsticks.

He shoos a fly from his bowl.

A morsel of pork drops from my grasp. He lifts it with his fingers, slips the fatty meat between my lips.

We become a crystal of salt, a crumb of sugar.

Late summer, time to feed our ancestors.

Do you believe in ghosts?

                        I believe in yours.

Heritage we're not sure we own. These
streets: Gore, Pender, Keefer – our craved
landscape. We spend afternoons at Sun Yat-
Sen Garden. Two Chinese parts, together –

We purchase a family membership.

We hold hands while Wayson Choy
discusses the unpredictability of life.
Impermanence. But you already know about
that, right? That's why you knead the soft of
my hand as if it is the last time.

Bloodlines – we are too thin for further dilution.

Flood the room. Bind me.

Half plus a half, we could deliver another ...

I split us into countries. One thinks, the
other lets the heart fester. One with hair
reaching like black tentacles, the other with
no hair at all.

We've broken into
lissom parts.

Phantom limbs
cannot touch
bodies.

How hard
to let go
of sameness.

Demi, hemi, semi – language between, we
understand. Customs, our own dialect,
letters chosen for shadows cast, shapes,
ways they can be misheard.

Separate, our tongues fade. Our hyphened
world –

As we untangle you dream of a Neil Young
concert in the basement of a building. You
look for me to let me know, but find only
my ghost and she says:

I am one
and half of you

You leave her to search for the real me –
wake to find me waiting for you, wet-eyed.

we drift

The sea heaves until we become water,
surge with eyes open.

Evaporation, I rise into the clouds. Now, I
can be a pillow, a tendril, a thunderstorm.

III

Music to accompany Section III, "The Sound of Waves":
talonbooks.com/OAHOY ♫

Wander where the water is salty enough to
turn corals pink, blush rocks. Conifers, and
trees hard to identify in the winter. Harbours
gleam, sleek lions guard buoys. Signals are
everywhere: lamps, lenses, day beacons, and
lanterns for charts incomplete. Pulses fade,
then reappear to keep something alive.
Swells and high gales – wonder the
frequency of seabird drownings.

Around me, bristly shoots, burrs. My fingers
stained by a grasshopper's acrid spit. Soil
under every nail. Hazy din of the train across
the inlet. Pitch softens, wood dries. Sun-
baked salt, seaweed, pine. Exoskeletons
disintegrate into minerals for the island.

From the salt marsh, pick segmented sea
bean tips – a succulent snap. Tongue the
brine. A brackish offering.

I breathe the tide, the sound of waves.

I dream
of amputation:
  my lover's arm.

My missing doesn't
thin.

Still I mill
stones between
molars.

Undamning what we
built.

If I sound desperate
I am.

I dive under sun to be torn by rocks and
barnacles, but suffer no loss of blood, feel
only aching sea. Seaweed like hands, my anchor.

I thought I'd forgotten my swimming sense
yet breaststroke to the knoll of kelp. There, I
think of you and moss, how you must have
dried.

I aim for the isle of birds – herons,
gulls, and geese – not caring I may not have
the strength, feet may not find bottom.

I make it, speak in breaths. Float until my
hair is salted. Jellyfish shadows on my arms
submerged.

Against a barnacled ridge, I look back to
shore.

Silt accretes. This is not failing. Anything
can be trapped. Sedimentary, layer upon
layer. Whole, but not perfect, animals will
die. Salt and sentiments collect in cracks.
Now we are bays.

I dream of finding you and my mouth opens
to pour jagged rocks.

Ravens follow
lengths I walk
call
          calling

mournful
          the Island never held you

bittersweet

here
          to sleep

with your ghost

denial
          when I extend
          and you are not there

so many seasons

I walk

ravens call   call
call
          and still

I walk back
          find seeds we piled
          forgot to plant

I water them

Vancouver's Chinatown lions defaced
with anti-Asian COVID ...

New "premium casual" plant-based
restaurant moving into ...

Another racially charged attack in
Vancouver's Chinatown

Racist graffiti scrawled on Chinatown
lions in Vancouver

For Chinatown Seniors, Survival
Means Staying in Touch

Chinatown businesses in city-owned
mall desperate for rent ...

Chinatown performance aims to
bring healing after racist ...

COVID-19: Series of anti-Asian
assaultsand vandalism ...

VPD report a 625% increase in anti-
Asian crime investigations ...

Anti-Asian hate crimes in Vancouver
not what veterans fought ...

Cat stuck on SkyTrain platform found
safe and sound, thanks ...

Bathing in the onsen, I notice my welts,
bruises, allergic reactions, freckles gone
wrong. Cuts I thought healed open with the
heat.

A decade of distance becomes bearable
until it isn't.

Everything is minerals – this water routed
from Yugawara up seven floors for us to
soak for our health with our breasts facing
the sea.

I'm unable to write a word
without you in my ink.

You, a part of me
apart from me.

From Japan to America, I mail you a
birthday card with an axolotl on the front.
Amphibious, dual-world dweller.

Only recently have I learned that this
salamander can regenerate limbs – possesses
the ability to heal itself.

Chinatown Supermarket on Keefer is
permanently closed. You wouldn't recognize
Main at Georgia, and did you hear about the
viaduct? Kam Gok Yuen was taken by fire.
The shop on Gore that sold cherimoyas and
holy basil disappeared after the rent
increased. On Pender: currywurst, coffee,
skateboards. An uncertain future. Even New
Town Bakery had a facelift. Displacement is
a pattern, not a single occurrence. Goldstone
with its oversized clock is newly gone
but of course Sun Yat-Sen Garden and the tourists
it brings are still there. Yes, there'll always be tourists.

Rat's body thickens, roots to earth. Sports
cars have given way to a Land Rover. He
and the blond model got married. Can you
believe it? Married. And now, children.

I will write Chinatown a poem, a love letter.

ACKNOWLEDGMENTS

This work exists thanks to the care from Kathleen, Madeleine, Dhana, Eleri, Tyler, Matea, Dawn, Alvin, Eliza, Merilyn, Phil, Betsy, TWS, and my family. With gratitude to Tom, for helping me make sense of things.

Thank you to Fred for your encouragement and support, to Cecily and Catriona for your enriching, generous insights, and the rest of the Talon team for bringing this book into the world.

With endless love and gratitude to Ritchie and BB.

And to Ryan – for love, music, and dreams.

Parts of this manuscript previously appeared in various forms in *Cha, QLRS, The Wild Weathers: a gathering of love poems* (Leaf Press), *Sustenance: Writers from BC and Beyond on the Subject of Food* (Anvil Press), *a fine. collection* (fine.press), *Poetry Is Dead, Plenitude, Cascadia Review, Room, Ricepaper, The Capilano Review, Science Creative Quarterly*, and *Accretion* and *Bitterzoet* "bonbon" chapbooks.

Page 76 is the Google News headline result for the search "Chinatown Vancouver" on May 31, 2020, and includes headlines from bc.ctvnews.ca, castanet.net, cbc.ca, globalnews.ca, straight.com, thetyee.ca, and vancouverisawesome.com.

All music written and performed by tidepools. Produced and recorded by Ryan Ogg. Mixed and mastered by Markus Reuter.

LEANNE DUNIC transgresses genres and form to produce projects such as *To Love the Coming End* (Book*hug / Chin Music Press, 2017) and *The Gift* (Book*hug, 2019). She is the leader of the band The Deep Cove, and lives on the unceded and occupied Traditional Territories of the xʷməθkʷəy̓əm, Sḵwx̱wú7mesh, and səl̓ilwətaɁɬ Peoples.

PHOTO: Dunic family archives